Session Objectives

After this session, you will be able to:

 Understand the value of your intellectual property to your export activities.

 Understand the FIVE basic steps you can take to secure and enforce your intellectual property in foreign markets.

 Locate U.S. Government resources that are available to assist you in protecting and enforcing your IP worldwide.

U.S. Department of Commerce | International Trade Administration

Intellectual Property in the U.S. Economy Report

- The entire U.S. economy relies on some form of IP, because virtually every industry either produces or uses it.

- IP-intensive industries accounted for over $5 trillion in value added, or almost 35% of U.S. gross domestic product (GDP), in 2010.

- Merchandise exports of these industries totaled $775 billion in 2010, accounting for 60.7% of total U.S. merchandise exports.

- In 2010, these industries directly and indirectly employed 40 million Americans, or 27.7% of all employment in the economy.

- Jobs in IP-intensive industries pay well compared to other jobs. Average weekly wages for IP-intensive industries were 42% higher than the average weekly wages in other (non-IP-intensive) private industries.

Intellectual Property in Pennsylvania

According to the Global Intellectual Property Center of the U.S. Chamber of Commerce:

- IP supports 2.54 million jobs, 48% of PA's private sector jobs.

- IP exports alone support nearly 247,000 jobs. That's because 75% of PA's exports were IP exports, worth nearly $31 billion.

- IP-intensive companies pay 29% higher than non-IP companies in PA.

- 3,961 patents were awarded to Pennsylvanians in 2013.

- Pennsylvania ranked 9th in the United States for R&D expenditures, spending $9.7 billion.

Step 1: Identify Your Company's Intellectual Property

Conduct an **IP audit**. Examine your business to see what might be eligible for a patent, trademark or copyright, or trade secret status.

STOPfakes.gov Resources

- Online IPR Training Module
- USPTO IP Awareness Assessment Tool

Step 2: Secure Rights in the United States

Companies should obtain IP rights in the U.S. by filing a patent application or registering their trademark or copyright with the proper U.S. Government Agencies.

- U.S. Patent and Trademark Office
  - www.uspto.gov; 1-800-786-9199
  - Patent $110-$850; Trademark $275-$375

- U.S. Copyright Office
  - www.copyright.gov
  - $35 (Electronic Filing)

Step 3: Secure Rights in Foreign Markets

Identify Export Markets

U.S. Export Assistance Center (USEAC) resources

- **Export.gov**: Trade Leads, Trade Events, Market Research, Other CS Resources

Consider ease of protecting and enforcing your IP

- Which markets are members of international IP agreements?
- Which markets have trade agreements with the United States that contain IP provisions?
- What are industries' major IP concerns in specific markets?

  - Annual Special 301 Report at www.ustr.gov

Step 3: Secure Rights in Foreign Markets

Where to protect your IPR: A Business Decision

- Where do you currently sell your product/service?

- Where do you want to sell your product/service in the future?

- Where are your products or components of your product produced?

- What are some of the more likely countries where infringement may occur?

Step 3: Secure Rights in Foreign Markets

STOPfakes.gov Resources:

- IPR Toolkits
- China Webinars
- IPR Attachés
- Country Commercial Guides (available from USEAC)
- Transatlantic IPR Portal with EU's China Help Desk

Step 3: Secure Rights in Foreign Markets

- <u>Trademarks:</u> The Madrid Agreement and Protocol
  - File international application with USPTO
  - 92 countries as of April 2014
  - www.WIPO.int; www.USPTO.gov

- <u>Patents:</u> The Patent Cooperation Treaty
  - File PCT application with U.S. Receiving Office at USPTO
  - 148 countries as of April 2014

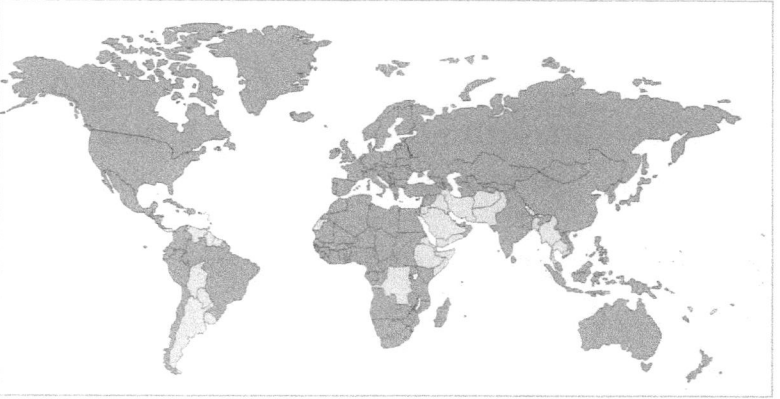

Step 3: Secure Rights in Foreign Markets

Register your copyrights.

- *As with trademark and patent,* there is **no such thing as an "international copyright"** that will automatically protect a work throughout the world. Protection against unauthorized use in a particular country depends on the national laws of that country.

- However, most countries offer protection to foreign works under certain conditions that have been greatly simplified by international copyright treaties and conventions such as the Berne Convention.

Step 4: Know Your Business Partners and Protect Your Trade Secrets

Know your potential business partners.

Do not assume that your business partner is looking out for your company's best interest.

- Consider using the Commercial Service's International Company Profile Service.

- Develop strong contractual relationships with your business partners, as those partners may be key to protecting your IP.

- Make sure <u>you</u> are registered as the owner of your IP, not your business partner.

Step 4: Know Your Business Partners and Protect Your Trade Secrets

Keep your trade secret a secret.

- A "trade secret" is usually defined in broad terms and includes:
    - sales methods
    - lists of suppliers and clients
    - manufacturing processes
    - consumer profiles
    - distribution methods
    - advertising strategies

- All WTO members are required to protect trade secrets, and many countries have laws that specifically protect trade secrets.

- Unfortunately, trade secret laws vary from country to country, are complex and often overlap with contract law and unfair competition law.

Step 4: Know Your Business Partners and Protect Your Trade Secrets

Keep your trade secret a secret.

Some general advice:

- Be extremely cautious about revealing too much information to business partners.

- Whenever possible, compartmentalize trade secrets so that no one employee has access to all of your proprietary information.

- Be on guard at trade shows and international expositions.

- Periodically review your security procedures, especially your cyber-security procedures.

Step 4: Know Your Business Partners and Protect Your Trade Secrets

Additional resources on trade secrets:

- The **White House** recently released the *Administration's Strategy on Mitigating the Theft of U.S. Trade Secrets*.

- The **World Intellectual Property Organization** has trade secret information specifically designed for small and medium-sized enterprises. *(www.WIPO.int)*

- **CREATe.org** offers guidance in a white paper titled *Trade Secret Theft: Managing the Growing Threat in Supply Chains* that includes:
    1. Conducting a strategic assessment of trade secrets;
    2. Undertaking appropriate pre-contractual due diligence;
    3. Employing strong contractual protections, backed by enforceable audit rights and penalties;
    4. Utilizing appropriate operational and security measures; and
    5. Ensuring appropriate action after a business relationship has ended.

Step 5: Enforce IPR at Home and Abroad

Companies must enforce their IPR.
Enforcement is first and foremost the right holder's responsibility!

Civil Remedies

- Cease & desist; notice & takedown
- Licensing agreements
- Lawsuits; alternative dispute resolution

Remedies at the Border

- Record with customs: https://apps.cbp.gov/e-recordations
- ITC Section 337 Investigations

Step 5: Enforce IPR at Home and Abroad

Criminal Remedies:

National IPR Coordination Center

- Visit www.iprcenter.gov and click on "Report IP Crimes" tab to file a report

- 1-866-IPR-2060; www.ice.gov

Step 5: Enforce IPR at Home and Abroad

In Foreign Markets...

- **Understand the options you will have in that market.**
  - IPR Toolkits
  - IPR Attachés
  - Country Commercial Guides

- **Talk with other U.S. companies and business associations in an effort to gain market insight.**

- **Develop a strategy of how you will deal with infringement of your intellectual property.**

Step 5: Enforce IPR at Home and Abroad

In Foreign Markets...

- Identify local attorneys, who specialize in local intellectual property rights law.
  - U.S. Commercial Service at U.S. Embassies can provide you with lists of local law firms.

- Record your rights with local customs, whenever possible.

- Proactively monitor the market to ensure that your IPR is not being infringed.

Quick Review

To Protect Itself from IPR Theft, a Company Should...

1. Conduct an IP Audit

2. Register IP in the U.S.

3. Register IP in Foreign Markets

4. Research Business Partners and Protect Trade Secrets

5. Enforce IPR at home and abroad

Ensuring Companies Benefit from U.S. Trade Agreements

- **Agreement on Trade Related Aspects of Intellectual Property Rights (TRIPs)**

- **World Intellectual Property Organization Internet Treaties (WPPT & WCT)**

- **FTAs (17):** Australia, Bahrain, Canada, Chile, Costa Rica, Dominican Republic, El Salvador, Guatemala, Honduras, Israel, Jordan, Mexico, Morocco, Nicaragua, Oman, Peru, Singapore
    - Recent FTAs: Colombia, Panama, Korea

- **Trade and Investment Framework Agreements & Bilateral Investment Treaties**

Ensuring Companies Benefit from U.S. Trade Agreements

When we identify unfair treatment:
- Meet with business
- Form a compliance team
- Craft an action plan
- Raise the issue with appropriate authorities

Experts in more than just IPR!

Case Study: Egypt

- **Problem:** The Egyptian Olympic Committee (EOC) sourced sports outfits for the 2012 Egyptian Olympic delegation from an unauthorized distributor selling counterfeit Nike uniforms.

- **Strategy:**
  - Commerce and U.S. Ambassadors to Egypt and the UK raised the issue with Egyptian trade and foreign affairs officials
  - Commerce facilitated dialogue between Nike and EOC officials

- **Result:** The EOC accepted genuine goods from Nike for the Egyptian athletes, and the Government of Egypt indicated it would open an investigation into the EOC procurement practices.

Please keep in touch...

Bijou Mgbojikwe

Office of Intellectual Property Rights

Industry and Analysis

U.S. Department of Commerce

202-482-1722

Bijou.Mgbojikwe@trade.gov